How to use your skill to launch a business:

The Creative's Guide to Starting a Business

BY

SIMEON FAVOUR

<u>**Index**</u>

"How to use your skill to launch a business: The Creative's Guide to Starting a Business" is a comprehensive guide tailored for creative individuals aspiring to turn their skills and passions into a successful business venture. This book provides practical advice, real-life examples, and actionable strategies to help creatives navigate the challenges of entrepreneurship while staying true to their artistic vision. Whether you're an artist, designer, writer, musician, or any other type of creative, this guide will empower you to launch and grow a thriving creative business.

Table of Contents

INTRODUCTION

In the vast realm of business, creativity is the driving force that ignites innovation, sparks change, and paves the way for groundbreaking ideas. Whether you're an artist, writer, designer, musician, or possess any creative skill, you hold within you the power to transform your passions into a thriving entrepreneurial venture. Welcome to "From Skill to Success: The Creative's Guide to Starting a Business." This book is your compass on a journey of self-discovery and entrepreneurial exploration.

The Entrepreneurial Journey

Every great venture begins with a single step, and your journey as a creative entrepreneur is no different. As you embark on this path, you are not merely starting a business; you are embarking on an adventure. The entrepreneurial journey is a rollercoaster of highs and lows, challenges and triumphs, setbacks and progress. It's a journey that will test your mettle, fuel your determination, and ultimately, reward your resilience.

In the chapters ahead, we will unravel the intricacies of entrepreneurship specifically tailored to the creative mind. You'll learn how to harness your talents, identify your unique value, and translate your artistic vision into a profitable venture. Along the way, you'll discover that the entrepreneurial path is a dynamic one, marked by constant learning, adaptability, and the cultivation of a growth mindset.

As we delve deeper into this journey, we'll explore the nuts and bolts of transforming your creative passion into a sustainable business. From crafting your brand identity to navigating the legalities of entrepreneurship, we'll provide you with the tools and knowledge you need to thrive.

Unleashing Your Creative Potential

Your creative potential is an untapped reservoir of ideas, inspiration, and innovation waiting to be unleashed. It's the wellspring from which your entrepreneurial journey flows. To unlock this potential, you must first believe in your abilities and recognize the value of your creative skills.

In the pages that follow, you'll learn not only how to harness your creativity but also how to channel it effectively into your business endeavors. Creativity is not a finite resource; the more you use it, the more it multiplies. We'll guide you through exercises and techniques to keep your creative juices flowing, even in the face of challenges.

Your creative potential is the cornerstone of your success as a creative entrepreneur. It's what sets you apart in a crowded marketplace, fuels your passion, and drives your business forward. By embracing your creative identity and nurturing your talents, you're not just embarking on a business venture; you're embarking on a transformative journey of self-discovery and self-empowerment.

This book is your companion, your mentor, and your source of inspiration on this extraordinary voyage. So, let's set sail together into the world of creative entrepreneurship, where your skills meet opportunity, and your passion finds purpose. Together, we will turn your creative dreams into a reality, one step at a time.

Chapter 1: Identifying Your Creative Skills

- **Recognizing Your Unique Talents**
- **Passion vs. Profit: Finding the Balance**

In the intricate tapestry of creative entrepreneurship, the very first thread you must unravel is the one that leads to self-discovery. To embark on this journey, you need to identify and understand your creative skills—those unique talents and abilities that set you apart from the rest. In this chapter, we'll delve into the art of recognizing your creative prowess and discuss the delicate balance between passion and profit. Here's how to navigate this path:

- ***Embrace Self-Awareness***: Self-awareness is the cornerstone of identifying your creative skills. Take the time to reflect on your life, your experiences, and your interests. Ask yourself probing questions: What do you enjoy doing in your free time? What activities make you lose track of time? When do you feel most in your element?

For example, if you find that you lose yourself in writing poetry, it could indicate a talent for linguistic creativity.
If you lose hours in front of a canvas, you might possess a talent for visual arts.

- ***Recall Childhood Passions***: Often, our childhood interests provide valuable clues to our innate talents. Think back to what you enjoyed doing as a child. Were you always doodling, making up stories, or putting on impromptu performances for your family? These early inclinations can reveal your creative calling.

- ***Analyze Feedback:*** Seek feedback from friends, family, teachers, or mentors. They may have observed talents in you that you didn't recognize. Honest conversations with those who know you well can provide fresh perspectives.

- ***Passion Projects***: Consider the projects you undertake purely out of passion, not for external validation or financial gain. These projects often align with your true creative self. Analyze why you are drawn to these endeavors and what they reveal about your interests and abilities.

- ***Skill Assessments***: Leverage online assessments and tools designed to identify creative strengths. These quizzes and tests can provide valuable insights into your abilities and preferences.

- ***Experiment and Explore***: Don't limit yourself to preconceived notions. Try your hand at various creative activities, even if you haven't explored them before. Sign up for a photography class, take up a musical instrument, or try your hand at sculpting. Experimentation can uncover latent talents.

- ***<u>Feedback Loop:</u>*** Continuously seek feedback as you experiment with different creative pursuits. Ask for constructive criticism from peers or mentors to understand where your strengths lie.

- ***<u>Document Your Journey:</u>*** Keep a journal or digital record of your creative exploration. Document your thoughts, experiences, and any discoveries about your skills. Over time, patterns may emerge that point you toward your true calling.

<u>Recognizing Your Unique Talents</u>

Every individual possesses a set of skills and talents that make them unique. As a creative, these skills manifest in your ability to bring ideas to life, to see the world through a different lens, and to express yourself in ways that others may not. However, recognizing your creative skills requires a deep dive into self-awareness and introspection.

- ***Self-Reflection***: Start by reflecting on your life experiences. What activities have consistently sparked your interest and enthusiasm? What are the hobbies or pastimes that you lose yourself in for hours? These moments of flow often hint at your natural talents.

- ***Feedback from Others***: Sometimes, those around you can see your talents more clearly than you can. Seek feedback from friends, family, mentors, or colleagues who can offer insight into what they perceive as your strengths.

- ***Passion Projects***: Think about the creative projects you've undertaken voluntarily, purely out of passion. What were they, and why did you choose them? Your choices in these endeavors can provide valuable clues about your creative inclinations.

- **_Skills Assessment_**: There are numerous online assessments and personality tests that can help identify your creative strengths. Consider taking some of these tests to gain a clearer picture of your abilities.

- **_Experimentation_**: Don't be afraid to try new things. Experiment with various creative pursuits, from painting to writing, music to photography. You might discover hidden talents along the way.

By recognizing your unique talents, you lay the foundation for your creative business. These skills will be the tools of your trade, the raw materials for your creative endeavors. Embrace them, nurture them, and use them to shape your entrepreneurial path.

Passion vs. Profit: Finding the Balance

While identifying your creative skills is crucial, it's equally important to consider the delicate balance between passion and profit. Many creatives grapple with the question of whether to pursue their passion wholeheartedly or to seek financial stability through more conventional means. The truth lies in finding harmony between the two.

- ***Passion as a Driver:*** Passion is the fuel that will keep you motivated and engaged in your creative endeavors. It's what makes your work authentic and compelling. However, it may not always translate directly into profit.

- ***Market Demand***: To create a successful creative business, you must assess the market demand for your skills and creations. Is there an audience willing to pay for what you offer? Research the market to understand if your passion aligns with viable business opportunities.

- ***Diversification***: Sometimes, you can find a middle ground by diversifying your creative pursuits. This allows you to balance your passion projects with more financially lucrative endeavors.

- ***Transitioning Gradually***: If you're torn between your passion and profit, consider transitioning into full-time entrepreneurship gradually. Start as a side hustler while maintaining your day job until your creative business gains traction.

- ***Financial Planning***: Develop a clear financial plan that outlines your income goals and expenses. This plan will help you make informed decisions about when and how to pursue your creative passion full-time.

Remember that finding the balance between passion and profit is a personal journey. It requires introspection, research, and thoughtful decision-making. Your creative skills are your unique assets, and they can lead you down a path of both fulfillment and financial success when approached with a clear understanding of their potential. In the chapters ahead, we'll explore how to leverage these skills to create a sustainable and prosperous creative business.

Chapter 2: Market Research and Validation

- Validating Your Creative Idea
- Navigating the Business Landscape
- Identifying Your Target Audience

In the realm of creative entrepreneurship, the path to success is paved with a dual commitment: staying true to your creative vision while meeting the demands and expectations of your target audience. Chapter 2, "Market Research and Validation," is your guide to navigating this delicate balance. Here, we'll explore the intricacies of understanding your market, identifying your target audience, and validating your creative idea. This chapter explores the crucial aspects of market research and validation, equipping you with the knowledge and tools to navigate the dynamic landscape of your creative business.

The Importance of Market Research

Market research is the process of gathering, analyzing, and interpreting information about your target market, industry, and potential customers. It's a fundamental step in understanding the context in which your creative business will operate. Here's why market research is essential:

- ***Informed Decision-Making***: Market research provides the data and insights needed to make informed decisions. It helps you assess the feasibility of your creative idea and tailor your approach to meet market needs.

- ***Identifying Opportunities and Threats***: By analyzing the market, you can identify opportunities for growth and potential threats or challenges that may arise. This foresight allows you to develop strategies to mitigate risks.

- ***Understanding Customer Needs***: Market research allows you to gain a deep understanding of your target audience's needs, preferences, and pain points. This knowledge is invaluable for crafting products or services that resonate with customers.

- ***Effective Marketing***: Armed with market insights, you can create targeted marketing campaigns that reach the right audience with the right message. This maximizes the efficiency of your marketing efforts.

- ***<u>Competitive Advantage</u>***: Market research helps you identify gaps in the market that your creative business can fill. This can give you a competitive advantage and help you stand out in a crowded marketplace.

- ***<u>Financial Planning</u>***: Accurate market data is essential for financial planning. It enables you to set realistic financial goals, pricing strategies, and revenue projections.

<u>The Process of Market Research</u>

Effective market research is a structured process that involves several key steps:

- ***<u>Define Your Objectives</u>***: Start by clearly defining your research objectives. What specific information do you need to gather, and what are your goals?

- ***Secondary Research***: Begin with secondary research, which involves collecting existing data and information from various sources, such as industry reports, publications, and online databases.

- ***Primary Research***: Conduct primary research to gather first hand data. This can involve surveys, interviews, focus groups, or observation. Primary research provides insights tailored to your unique needs.

- ***Analyze Data***: Analyze the data collected from both secondary and primary research. Look for patterns, trends, and insights that can inform your business strategy.

- ***Identify Your Unique Selling Proposition (USP)***: Based on your research findings, identify what sets your creative business apart from competitors.

This is your Unique Selling Proposition (USP).

- ***Target Market Segmentation***: Segment your target market based on demographic, psychographic, or behavioral factors. This segmentation helps you tailor your offerings to specific customer groups.

- ***Competitor Analysis***: Analyze your competitors' strengths, weaknesses, strategies, and customer reviews. Understanding your competition is critical for differentiation.

- ***Legal and Regulatory Considerations***: Be aware of any legal or regulatory requirements that may apply to your creative business. Ensure compliance from the outset.

VALIDATING YOUR CREATIVE IDEA

Market validation is the process of confirming that there is a genuine demand for your creative product or service. It's about verifying that your idea aligns with market needs and preferences. Here's why validation matters:

- ***Risk Mitigation***: Validation minimizes the risk of investing time and resources in an idea that may not succeed in the market.

- ***Confidence Building:*** A validated idea provides you with confidence that you are on the right track and that there is a receptive audience for your creative work.

- ***Resource Allocation***: It helps you allocate resources more efficiently, focusing on ideas that have a higher likelihood of success.

<u>**Methods of Validation**</u>

Several methods can be employed to validate your creative idea:

- ***<u>Surveys and Questionnaires</u>***: Create surveys or questionnaires to gather feedback from your target audience. Ask about their interest in your concept and whether they would be willing to pay for it.

- ***<u>Prototyping</u>***: Develop a prototype or sample of your creative work and present it to potential customers or focus groups to gauge their reactions and interest.

- ***<u>Market Testing</u>***: Launch a small-scale version of your product or service to a select group of customers. Monitor their response and gather feedback.

- ***<u>Competitive Analysis:</u>*** Analyze similar offerings in the market. If comparable ideas are thriving, it's a positive indicator for your concept.

- ***<u>Crowdfunding Campaigns:</u>*** Run a crowdfunding campaign to gauge interest and secure initial funding. The level of support can indicate market demand.

- ***<u>Pilot Programs</u>***: Implement a pilot program to test your idea in a real-world setting with a limited audience before a full-scale launch.

- ***<u>Feedback and Iteration</u>***: Continuously seek and incorporate feedback from potential customers to refine your creative idea.

<u>Navigating the Business Landscape</u>

As a creative entrepreneur, you're stepping into a dynamic and competitive business landscape. To thrive in this environment, you need to gain a comprehensive understanding of the market you're entering. Navigating the business landscape involves several crucial steps:

- ***Market Analysis***: Begin by conducting a thorough market analysis. Research your industry, competitors, and trends. Understand the current state of the market and any opportunities or gaps that exist.

- ***SWOT Analysis***: Perform a SWOT analysis—assess your **strengths**, **weaknesses, opportunities**, and **threats**. This exercise helps you identify your competitive advantages and potential challenges.

- ***Competitor Research***: Study your competitors closely. Analyze their products or services, pricing strategies, marketing efforts, and customer reviews. What can you learn from their successes and failures?

- ***<u>Market Trends:</u>*** Stay up-to-date with industry trends and emerging technologies. This knowledge will enable you to adapt and innovate within your field.

- ***<u>Legal and Regulatory Considerations</u>***: Be aware of any legal or regulatory requirements that may impact your creative business. This includes licensing, permits, copyright, and trademark considerations.

- ***<u>Risk Assessment</u>***: Assess the risks associated with your business, both financial and operational. Develop strategies to mitigate these risks.

- ***<u>Business Models:</u>*** Explore different business models within your industry. Are there established models you can adopt, or is there room for innovation?

By thoroughly navigating the business landscape, you gain a strategic advantage. You'll be better prepared to make informed decisions and position your creative business effectively.

Identifying Your Target Audience

To thrive as a creative entrepreneur, you must understand and connect with your target audience—the individuals or groups most likely to appreciate and invest in your creative offerings. Identifying your target audience involves the following steps:

- ***Create Buyer Personas***: Develop detailed buyer personas that represent your ideal customers. Consider factors such as demographics, interests, pain points, and purchasing behavior.

- ***Market Segmentation***: Segment your market based on common characteristics.

Are there specific niches or segments within your industry that align with your creative vision?

- ***<u>Survey and Research:</u>*** Conduct surveys, interviews, or focus groups to gather insights directly from your target audience. What are their needs, preferences, and challenges?

- ***<u>Competitor Analysis</u>***: Analyze the target audience of your competitors. Are there underserved or overlooked segments that you can target?

- ***<u>Online Tools:</u>*** Utilize online tools and platforms, such as social media analytics and Google Analytics, to gather data on your audience's online behavior.

- ***<u>Feedback Loops</u>***: Create feedback loops with your existing customers. Their insights can help refine your understanding of your target audience.

- ***Value Proposition***: Craft a compelling value proposition that speaks directly to the needs and desires of your target audience. What unique benefits do your creative products or services offer?

Understanding your target audience is a continuous process. As market dynamics evolve, so do the preferences and needs of your audience. By staying attuned to these changes, you can tailor your creative offerings to maintain relevance and appeal.

Chapter 3: Crafting a Unique Value Proposition

- Defining Your Unique Selling Points
- Creating a Compelling Brand Story

In the world of creative entrepreneurship, your value proposition is your promise to your customers. It's the unique blend of benefits and characteristics that sets your creative business apart from the competition. In this chapter, we'll explore the art of crafting a unique value proposition, defining your unique selling points, and creating a compelling brand story. Here's a more detailed look at the steps involved:

Step 1: Understand Your Target Audience
Before you can craft a compelling UVP, you must have a deep understanding of your target audience. Consider the following:

- ***Demographics***: Who are your ideal customers? Age, gender, location, income level, and other demographic factors can shape your UVP.

- ***Psychographics***: What are their values, interests, and behaviors? Understanding their motivations and aspirations is crucial.

- ***Pain Points***: What problems or challenges do they face that your creative product or service can solve? Addressing these pain points can be a key component of your UVP.

- ***Desires and Goals:*** What are their desires, goals, and aspirations? Your UVP should align with and appeal to these.

Step 2: Identify Your Unique Selling Points (USPs)

Your USPs are the specific attributes or benefits that make your creative business stand out from the competition. These could include:

- ***Unique Features***: Is there something distinct about your products or services that no one else offers? It could be a unique technique, style, or material you use.

- ***<u>Quality</u>***: If your creative work is known for its exceptional quality, this can be a compelling USP.

- ***<u>Innovation</u>***: Are you pushing boundaries and introducing new concepts or styles to your field? Innovation can set you apart.

- ***<u>Customer Experience</u>***: Exceptional customer service, personalization, or a seamless buying experience can be a strong USP.

- ***<u>Sustainability</u>***: If your creative business is committed to eco-friendly practices, this can resonate with environmentally conscious consumers.

- ***<u>Heritage or Story</u>***: A compelling origin story or a deep connection to a particular culture or tradition can be a unique selling point.

Step 3: Define the Benefit or Value You Offer

Your UVP should clearly communicate the benefit or value that customers will derive from your creative products or services. This should answer the question, "What's in it for the customer?" Consider:

- **_Solving a Problem_**: If your creative work addresses a specific problem or need, highlight how it does so effectively.

- **_Emotional Connection:_** If your creations evoke strong emotions or memories, emphasize the emotional impact on customers.

- **_Enhancing Life_**: Explain how your products or services can improve or enhance the lives of your customers.

- ***<u>Saving Time or Effort</u>***: If your offerings save customers time, effort, or stress, make this a prominent part of your UVP.

- ***<u>Uniqueness</u>***: Reinforce the unique aspects of your creative work and how they differentiate you from the competition.

<u>Step 4: Keep It Clear and Concise</u>

Your UVP should be succinct and easy to understand. Aim for a concise statement or tagline that encapsulates your unique value. Avoid jargon or overly technical language that may confuse your audience.

<u>Step 5: Test and Refine</u>

Once you've crafted your UVP, test it with your target audience. Seek feedback to ensure that it resonates with them and effectively communicates your value. Be open to refining your UVP based on this feedback.

Step 6: Integrate Your UVP Across Touchpoints

Your UVP should be consistently integrated into all aspects of your branding and marketing efforts. This includes your website, social media profiles, marketing materials, and even your interactions with customers.

Step 7: Monitor and Adapt

Market conditions and customer preferences can change over time. Continuously monitor the effectiveness of your UVP and be prepared to adapt it to stay relevant and competitive.

Defining Your Unique Selling Points

Your unique selling points (USPs) are the distinct qualities, features, or attributes that make your creative business stand out in the eyes of your target audience. These are the reasons why customers should choose your products or services over others. Here's how to define your USPs:

- ***<u>Identify Your Strengths:</u>*** Begin by identifying the strengths of your creative business. What do you excel at? Is it your artistic talent, your innovative approach, or your commitment to sustainability?

- ***<u>Analyze Competitors:</u>*** Conduct a competitive analysis to understand what your competitors offer. Then, pinpoint the gaps or areas where your creative business can excel.

- ***<u>Unique Features or Benefits</u>***: Consider the unique features or benefits of your products or services. What makes them different or better than alternatives in the market?

- ***<u>Customer Pain Points</u>***: Identify the pain points or challenges that your target audience faces. How does your creative offering address or solve these issues?

- ***Customer Feedback:*** Gather feedback from existing customers or potential customers. What do they value most about your creative work? Use their insights to refine your USPs.

- ***Value Metrics:*** Determine the metrics by which customers can measure the value of your offerings. This could be quality, affordability, sustainability, uniqueness, or any other relevant criterion.

- ***Emotional Connection***: Consider the emotional connection your creative work fosters. Does it evoke strong emotions or resonate with a particular lifestyle or ethos?

- ***Storytelling***: Weave your USPs into a compelling narrative that communicates not only what you offer but also why it matters. This narrative will be a critical component of your brand story.

Crafting compelling USPs requires a deep understanding of your creative business, your customers, and the competitive landscape. Your USPs should not only be unique but also resonate with your target audience's needs and desires.

Creating a Compelling Brand Story

A brand story is more than just a marketing tactic; it's the soul of your creative business. It communicates your mission, values, and identity to your audience. Here's how to create a compelling brand story:

- ***Define Your Brand Identity***: Begin by defining your brand identity. What does your creative business stand for? What are your core values, and how do they align with your creative work?

- ***Origin Story:*** Share the story of how your creative business came into being. What inspired you to pursue your creative passion? Your origin story can humanize your brand and create a connection with customers.

- ***Mission and Vision:*** Clearly articulate your mission and vision. What impact do you want to make with your creative work? How do you envision the future of your business?

- ***Values and Beliefs***: Communicate the values and beliefs that underpin your creative work. What do you stand for, and what principles guide your decisions and actions?

- ***Customer-Centric***: Highlight the role of your customers in your brand story. Showcase how your creative work enriches their lives, addresses their needs, or solves their problems.

- ***Authenticity***: Be authentic in your storytelling. Authenticity builds trust and credibility with your audience. Share both successes and challenges in your creative journey.

- ***Visual and Verbal Identity***: Your brand story should be reflected in your visual identity (logo, design, colors) and your verbal identity (brand messaging, tone of voice).

- ***Consistency***: Ensure consistency in how you communicate your brand story across all touchpoints, from your website to social media and marketing materials.

- ***Engagement and Connection***: Encourage engagement and connection with your brand story. Invite customers to be a part of your narrative and share their experiences with your creative products or services.

A compelling brand story goes beyond marketing; it becomes a powerful tool for building a community of loyal customers who resonate with your creative vision. It's the emotional bridge that connects your audience to your creative business, fostering lasting relationships.

In this chapter, we've explored the significance of crafting a unique value proposition, defining your unique selling points, and creating a compelling brand story. These elements will not only set your creative business apart but also form the foundation upon which you build a strong and enduring brand presence in the market.

Chapter 4: Building a Strong Brand

- Branding Essentials for Creatives
- The Importance of Consistency

In the creative world of entrepreneurship, your brand is your signature, your identity, and your promise to your audience. In this chapter, we'll explore the essentials of building a strong brand for your creative business. We'll discuss branding essentials for creatives and the paramount importance of consistency. This chapter dives into the essential principles and steps to build a robust brand for your creative business.

1. Define Your Brand Identity

Your brand identity is the essence of who you are as a creative business. It encompasses your values, personality, and the unique qualities that set you apart. Start by:

- ***<u>Defining Your Values</u>***: What principles and beliefs guide your creative work? Your values should resonate with your target audience.

- ***<u>Identifying Your Personality</u>***: Is your brand playful, sophisticated, or adventurous? Your brand's personality should align with your creative style.

- ***<u>Uncovering Your Purpose</u>***: Why does your creative business exist? Beyond making a profit, what impact do you aspire to create in the world?

<u>2. Craft a Distinct Visual Identity</u>

Your visual identity is the face of your brand. It includes your logo, color palette, typography, and design elements. When designing your visual identity:

- ***<u>Logo Design</u>***: Create a memorable and versatile logo that encapsulates your brand's spirit. It should be simple yet distinctive.

- ***Color Psychology***: Choose colors that evoke the desired emotions and associations. Colors have a profound impact on how your brand is perceived.

- ***Typography***: Select fonts that reflect your brand's personality. Typography can convey a sense of professionalism, creativity, or elegance.

- ***Design Elements***: Consistency in design elements, such as patterns or graphics, reinforces your brand's visual identity.

3. Develop Your Brand Voice and Messaging

Your brand voice is the tone and style in which you communicate with your audience. Your messaging should be:

- ***Consistent***: Maintain a consistent voice across all channels, from your website to social media. Consistency builds brand recognition.

- ***Authentic***: Be genuine in your communication. Authenticity fosters trust and resonates with audiences.

- ***Audience-Centric***: Tailor your messaging to the needs, interests, and preferences of your target audience.

- ***Storytelling***: Share your brand's story, weaving in your journey, values, and mission. Storytelling creates emotional connections.

4. Prioritize Consistency

Consistency is the bedrock upon which strong brands are built. Ensure that your brand elements, voice, and messaging remain consistent across all touchpoints. This consistency extends to:

- ***Visuals***: Maintain a uniform visual identity in all materials, from your website and social media profiles to marketing collateral.

- ***Messaging***: Use the same tone, style, and key messages in your communications.

- ***Customer Experience***: Consistency in the quality of your creative work and the customer experience fosters trust and loyalty.

5. Connect Emotionally with Your Audience

Emotional connections create loyal customers. Strive to:

- ***Evoke Emotions:*** Craft creative work that elicits emotions, whether it's joy, nostalgia, or inspiration.

- ***<u>Engage Authentically</u>***: Interact with your audience authentically. Respond to comments and messages personally.

- ***<u>Tell Relatable Stories</u>***: Share stories and experiences that resonate with your audience's aspirations and challenges.

<u>6. Be Customer-Centric</u>

Your customers are at the heart of your brand's success. Be customer-centric by:

- ***<u>Listening Actively</u>***: Solicit feedback and actively listen to your customers' opinions and needs.

- ***<u>Solve Problems</u>***: Address customer concerns promptly and effectively. A brand that solves problems builds trust.

- ***<u>Deliver Value</u>***: Continually deliver value through your creative products or services.

7. Evolve and Adapt

A strong brand is not static; it evolves with your creative business. Stay attuned to market trends, customer feedback, and changing circumstances. Adapt your brand as needed while staying true to your core identity.

8. Measure and Evaluate

Regularly assess the effectiveness of your branding efforts. Use metrics and customer feedback to gauge how well your brand resonates with your audience. Be open to adjustments and refinements based on these insights.

Building a strong brand is a dynamic process that requires dedication and a deep understanding of your creative business and audience. When executed effectively, your brand becomes a magnet, attracting loyal customers who not only appreciate your creative work but also connect with the values and personality that define your brand.

Branding Essentials for Creatives

- ***Visual Identity***: Your visual identity includes your logo, color palette, typography, and design elements. These elements should be carefully chosen to reflect your creative style and resonate with your target audience. Your visual identity is often the first impression you make on potential customers, so it should be memorable and aligned with your brand's values.

- ***Brand Name***: Your brand name should be unique, relevant to your creative niche, and easy to remember. It's the name that customers will associate with your creative work, so choose it thoughtfully.

- ***Tagline***: A well-crafted tagline can succinctly communicate your brand's essence and value. It should be memorable and encapsulate what sets your creative business apart.

- ***Storytelling***: Storytelling is a potent tool for creatives. Share your brand's story, including its origins, mission, and the passion that drives your creative work. Authentic and compelling storytelling can forge deep connections with your audience.

- ***Consistency in Messaging***: Consistency in your brand messaging ensures that your values, mission, and personality are conveyed cohesively across all communication channels. Whether it's your website, social media, or marketing materials, maintain a consistent voice and message.

- ***<u>Customer Experience</u>***: The experience customers have when interacting with your brand is crucial. From the moment they discover your creative work to the post-purchase experience, every touchpoint should reflect your brand's values and commitment to quality.

- ***<u>Brand Guidelines</u>***: Create brand guidelines that detail how your brand should be represented visually and verbally. This document ensures that anyone involved with your brand, from designers to content creators, maintains consistency in its presentation.

- ***<u>Unique Selling Proposition (USP):</u>*** Your USP, as discussed in the previous chapter, is a fundamental element of your brand. It should be clearly communicated in your branding to highlight what makes your creative work special.

- ***Emotional Connection:*** Successful branding often forges an emotional connection with customers. Identify the emotions you want your brand to evoke and design your branding elements accordingly.

- ***Feedback Loop***: Be open to feedback from your audience. Their input can help you refine your branding and ensure that it resonates with them.

The Importance of Consistency

Consistency is the bedrock of a strong brand. Here's why it's so crucial:

- ***Recognition***: Consistency in visual elements like logos and colors helps customers recognize your brand quickly. This recognition builds trust and loyalty over time.

- ***Professionalism***: A consistent brand presence conveys professionalism and reliability. It shows that you take your creative business seriously.

- ***Clarity***: Consistency in messaging and tone of voice ensures that your brand's values and mission are clear to your audience.

- ***Memorability***: A consistent brand is more likely to be remembered. When customers have a clear and consistent experience with your brand, they are more likely to recall it when making purchasing decisions.

- ***Credibility***: Consistency builds credibility. When customers see a brand that is cohesive and reliable, they are more likely to trust it.

- ***Differentiation***: In a crowded marketplace, consistency can help your brand stand out. It reinforces what makes your creative business unique.

- ***Customer Loyalty***: Consistency in the quality of your creative work and the customer experience fosters loyalty. Customers know what to expect, and if they consistently have positive experiences, they are more likely to become repeat buyers and advocates for your brand.

- ***Adaptability***: A consistent brand can adapt to changing market conditions while maintaining its core identity. It can introduce new products or services without losing its brand essence.

- ***Brand Equity***: Over time, consistency builds brand equity. This intangible asset represents the value and strength of your brand in the marketplace.

To maintain consistency in your brand, create and adhere to brand guidelines that dictate how your brand should be presented visually and verbally. Regularly review and update these guidelines as your creative business evolves.

In this chapter, you've explored the foundational elements of building a strong brand for your creative business. From visual identity to storytelling and the importance of consistency, these elements collectively shape how your brand is perceived and remembered by your audience. A strong brand can be a driving force in the success of your creative entrepreneurship.

Chapter 5: Business Planning and Strategy

- The Creative Business Plan
- Setting Realistic Goals
- Financial Planning for Creatives

In the world of creative entrepreneurship, a solid business plan and strategic thinking are the compass that guides your creative journey. In this chapter, we'll delve into the essentials of crafting a creative business plan, setting realistic goals, and navigating financial planning tailored to the unique needs of creatives. This chapter explores the crucial aspects of developing a creative business plan and crafting a strategic approach that aligns with your creative goals.

The Creative Business Plan

A creative business plan is your roadmap to turning your creative skills into a thriving venture. It serves as a blueprint for your creative journey, helping you articulate your vision and chart a course to achieve it. Here's how to create a comprehensive creative business plan:

- ***Executive Summary:*** Begin with a concise executive summary that encapsulates the essence of your creative business. It should provide a snapshot of your mission, unique selling points, and goals.

- ***Business Description***: Describe your creative business in detail. Explain your creative niche, the products or services you offer, and the problem or need your creative work addresses.

- ***Market Analysis***: Conduct a thorough analysis of your target market, industry trends, and competitors. Understand your audience's demographics, preferences, and pain points.

- ***Marketing and Sales Strategy***: Outline your marketing and sales approach. Define your branding strategy, advertising methods, and how you plan to acquire and retain customers.

- ***Product or Service Line***: Detail your creative offerings, emphasizing their unique features and benefits. Include pricing strategies and plans for product/service development or expansion.

- ***Operational Plan***: Describe the day-to-day operations of your creative business. Explain how you'll produce, deliver, and manage your creative work.

- ***Management and Team***: Introduce your team members, their roles, and their qualifications. Highlight your own expertise as the founder.

- ***Financial Projections***: Present financial projections, including income statements, balance sheets, and cash flow forecasts. Include a budget that covers startup costs and ongoing expenses.

- ***Funding Needs***: If you require funding, specify the amount and its purpose. Detail your funding sources, whether they're personal savings, loans, investors, or grants.

- ***Risk Analysis***: Identify potential risks and challenges your creative business may face. Develop strategies to mitigate these risks.

- ***Timeline***: Create a timeline that outlines key milestones and deadlines, from your business launch to growth stages.

Crafting Your Business Strategy

Once your creative business plan is in place, it's time to develop a strategic approach that will guide your day-to-day operations and long-term growth. Consider these strategic elements:

- **<u>Mission and Vision</u>**: Revisit your mission and vision regularly. They should guide every decision and action within your creative business.

- **<u>Unique Selling Proposition (USP)</u>**: Leverage your USP to differentiate your creative business in the market. Ensure your USP is consistently communicated in all marketing and branding efforts.

- **<u>Market Positioning</u>**: Position your creative business strategically in the market. Determine whether you'll compete based on price, quality, innovation, or another factor.

- **<u>Target Audience</u>**: Continuously refine your understanding of your target audience. Tailor your products, services, and marketing to meet their evolving needs and preferences.

- **<u>Brand Development</u>**: Nurture and evolve your brand identity. Your brand should reflect the core values and personality of your creative business.

- **<u>Marketing and Promotion</u>**: Implement a well-defined marketing strategy that includes online and offline channels. Regularly analyze the effectiveness of your marketing efforts and adapt as needed.

- **<u>Customer Experience</u>**: Prioritize delivering exceptional customer experiences. Happy customers become brand advocates and repeat buyers.

- **<u>Partnerships and Collaborations</u>**: Explore partnerships and collaborations with other creative professionals or businesses that align with your brand and can expand your reach.

- **<u>Innovation and Adaptation</u>**: Stay agile and open to innovation. Be ready to adapt to changing market conditions and customer preferences.

- **<u>Measuring Success</u>**: Define key performance indicators (KPIs) to track your progress. Regularly evaluate your performance against these metrics and adjust your strategy accordingly.

- **<u>Continuous Learning</u>**: Invest in your own professional development and stay informed about industry trends and best practices.

Business planning and strategic thinking are ongoing processes. Regularly revisit and revise your creative business plan and strategy as your business evolves. Flexibility and adaptability are key in the ever-changing landscape of creative entrepreneurship.

<u>Setting Realistic Goals</u>

Setting clear and achievable goals is pivotal for the success of your creative business. Follow these principles when setting goals:

- ***Specific***: Define your goals with precision. Avoid vague objectives like "increase sales." Instead, specify "increase monthly sales by 20%."

- ***Measurable***: Ensure that you can measure progress and success. Use quantifiable metrics, such as revenue, customer acquisition, or website traffic.

- ***Achievable***: Set goals that are challenging but realistic. Assess your resources, capabilities, and constraints to determine feasibility.

- ***Relevant***: Align your goals with your creative business's mission and overall strategy. Each goal should contribute to your business's growth and success.

- ***Time-Bound:*** Establish deadlines for achieving your goals. Having a timeframe creates a sense of urgency and accountability.

- ***Prioritize***: Focus on a few key goals at a time. Trying to achieve too many objectives simultaneously can lead to inefficiency and overwhelm.

- ***Track Progress***: Regularly monitor and evaluate your progress toward your goals. Adjust your strategy as needed to stay on track.

Financial Planning for Creatives

Financial planning is a critical aspect of managing a creative business. Consider the following financial planning principles:

- ***Budgeting***: Create a comprehensive budget that includes all business expenses, such as production costs, marketing expenses, and overhead. Budgeting helps you allocate resources efficiently.

- ***Cash Flow Management:*** Manage your cash flow effectively to ensure you have the funds needed to cover expenses and seize opportunities. Monitor your receivables and payables closely.

- ***Pricing Strategy:*** Determine the appropriate pricing strategy for your creative products or services. Consider factors like production costs, market demand, and perceived value.

- ***Revenue Streams:*** Explore diverse revenue streams. In addition to your core creative offerings, consider complementary products, services, or licensing opportunities.

- ***<u>Emergency Fund:</u>*** Maintain an emergency fund to cover unexpected expenses or periods of low income. Having a financial safety net provides peace of mind.

- ***<u>Financial Software</u>***: Use accounting and financial software to track income and expenses accurately. Consider consulting with a financial advisor or accountant for expert guidance.

- ***<u>Tax Planning:</u>*** Understand your tax obligations as a creative entrepreneur. Proper tax planning can help you maximize deductions and minimize liabilities.

- ***<u>Invest in Growth:</u>*** Allocate a portion of your income toward investments that can fuel the growth of your creative business, such as marketing campaigns or expanding your product line.

- ***<u>Retirement Planning:</u>*** Don't overlook retirement planning. Consider setting up retirement accounts or investments to secure your financial future.

- ***<u>Review and Adjust:</u>*** Regularly review your financial statements and adjust your financial strategy based on your business's performance and changing circumstances.

Crafting a creative business plan, setting realistic goals, and implementing sound financial planning are pivotal steps in the journey of creative entrepreneurship. These elements provide a structured framework for turning your creative passion into a thriving and sustainable business venture.

Chapter 6: Legalities and Business Structure

- Choosing the Right Legal Structure
- Navigating Intellectual Property
- Licensing and Copyright

In the realm of creative entrepreneurship, understanding the legal aspects of your creative business is vital to protect your work and navigate the complexities of the industry. In this chapter, we'll explore the importance of choosing the right legal structure, the nuances of intellectual property, and the significance of licensing and copyright. This chapter explores the importance of selecting the right legal structure, understanding intellectual property, and managing licensing and copyright.

Choosing the Right Legal Structure

Selecting the appropriate legal structure for your creative business is a fundamental decision that can have significant implications for your operations, taxes, and liability. Here are some common legal structures to consider:

- ***Sole Proprietorship***: This is the simplest form of business ownership, where you operate as an individual. While it's easy to set up, it offers no personal liability protection, meaning your personal assets are at risk in case of business-related issues.

- ***Partnership***: If you're collaborating with others, a partnership allows shared ownership and responsibilities. However, similar to sole proprietorships, partners have unlimited personal liability.

- ***Limited Liability Company (LLC)***: An LLC provides personal liability protection while offering flexibility in terms of management and taxation. It's a popular choice for small creative businesses.

- ***Corporation***: Corporations offer the highest level of liability protection but involve more complex legal and administrative requirements. They are suitable for larger creative businesses looking to raise capital.

- ***Nonprofit***: If your creative work has a charitable or social mission, consider forming a nonprofit organization. Nonprofits have tax benefits but are subject to strict regulations.

- ***Cooperative***: A cooperative structure allows multiple stakeholders, such as artists or creators, to collectively own and manage the business for mutual benefit.

The choice of legal structure should align with your business goals, size, and risk tolerance.

Consulting with legal and financial professionals can help you make an informed decision.

<u>Understanding Intellectual Property (IP)</u>

Intellectual property (IP) is at the core of creative entrepreneurship, protecting your creative works and ideas. Here are the main categories of IP:

- ***<u>Copyright</u>***: Copyright protects original creative works such as literature, music, visual art, and software. Registering your copyright strengthens your ability to enforce your rights.

- ***<u>Trademark</u>***: Trademarks safeguard brand names, logos, and symbols associated with your creative business. Registering a trademark prevents others from using similar marks.

- ***Patents***: Patents protect unique inventions, processes, and designs. If your creative work involves innovative technologies or inventions, consider patent protection.

- ***Trade Secrets:*** Trade secrets encompass confidential business information, like formulas, processes, or customer lists. Implement robust security measures to protect trade secrets.

- ***Public Domain***: Works in the public domain are not protected by copyright and can be used freely. Ensure you have the right to use materials before incorporating them into your creative work.

Licensing and Copyright Management

Licensing and copyright management are crucial aspects of creative entrepreneurship:

- ***Licensing***: Licensing allows you to grant others permission to use your creative work under specific terms and conditions. It's a valuable revenue source for creatives.

- ***Copyright Infringement***: Vigilantly monitor your copyrighted work for unauthorized use. Take legal action if infringement occurs to protect your rights.

- ***License Agreements***: When licensing your work, create clear and comprehensive license agreements that detail usage rights, royalties, restrictions, and duration.

- ***Fair Use***: Understand fair use provisions, which allow limited use of copyrighted material without permission for purposes like criticism, commentary, or education.

- ***Work for Hire***: Clearly define work-for-hire agreements when collaborating with others to specify ownership and rights to creative work.

- ***Moral Rights***: Some jurisdictions recognize moral rights that protect the integrity of your creative work, even if you've transferred copyright.

- ***Creative Commons***: Consider using Creative Commons licenses to specify how others can use your work while retaining certain rights.

Navigating the legalities and business structure of your creative endeavor requires careful consideration and professional guidance. Consult with intellectual property attorneys and legal experts to ensure that your creative assets are protected and that you comply with relevant laws and regulations.

Choosing the Right Legal Structure

Selecting the appropriate legal structure for your creative business is a critical decision that impacts liability, taxes, and management. Here are common legal structures to consider:

- ***Sole Proprietorship***: This is the simplest form, where you are the sole owner and responsible for all aspects of the business. It offers full control but exposes you to personal liability.

- ***Partnership***: If you're collaborating with others, a partnership structure allows shared ownership and responsibilities. However, partners share profits and liabilities.

- ***Limited Liability Company (LLC): An*** LLC provides personal liability protection while allowing flexibility in management and taxation. It's a popular choice for creative businesses.

- ***Corporation***: Corporations offer the highest level of liability protection but involve more complex formalities. They can be advantageous for raising capital or long-term growth.

- ***Nonprofit***: If your creative work has a social or charitable focus, consider forming a nonprofit organization. It has tax benefits but comes with strict regulations.

- ***Cooperative***: A cooperative structure allows multiple stakeholders, such as artists or creators, to collectively own and manage the business for mutual benefit.

Choosing the right legal structure depends on your goals, the scale of your creative business, and the level of control and protection you desire. Consult with legal and financial advisors to make an informed decision.

Navigating Intellectual Property

Intellectual property (IP) is at the heart of creative entrepreneurship. Understanding and protecting your IP rights is essential. Here are the main categories of IP:

- ***Copyright***: Protects original creative works, including literature, music, visual art, and software. Register your copyright to enforce your rights more effectively.

- ***Trademark***: Trademarks safeguard brand names, logos, and symbols associated with your creative business. Registering a trademark prevents others from using similar marks.

- ***Patents***: Patents protect inventions, processes, and designs. If your creative work involves unique inventions or technologies, consider patent protection.

- ***Trade Secrets:*** Trade secrets encompass confidential business information, such as formulas, processes, or customer lists.

Implement robust confidentiality measures to safeguard trade secrets.

Public Domain: Works in the public domain are not protected by copyright and can be used freely. Ensure you have the right to use materials before incorporating them into your creative work.

In this chapter, you've explored the significance of choosing the right legal structure, understanding intellectual property, and effectively managing licensing and copyright in the world of creative entrepreneurship. These legal considerations are integral to safeguarding your creative work and building a strong foundation for your creative business.

Chapter 7: Funding Your Creative Venture

- Bootstrapping vs. External Funding

Funding your creative venture is a pivotal step in turning your creative passion into a successful business. This chapter explores the choices you have, from bootstrapping to seeking external funding, and the various funding options available for creative businesses. Here are the key steps to crafting a creative portfolio that makes a lasting impression:

1. Define Your Purpose and Audience:

- ***Purpose***: Determine the primary purpose of your portfolio. Are you seeking freelance work, applying for jobs, attracting clients, or showcasing personal projects? Clarify your goals.

- ***Audience***: Understand your target audience. Tailor your portfolio to the preferences and needs of potential clients, employers, or collaborators.

2. Select Your Best Work:

- ***Quality Over Quantity***: Choose a selection of your highest-quality work. It's better to have a smaller number of outstanding pieces than a large quantity of mediocre ones.

Variety: Showcase a diverse range of projects that demonstrate your skills, style, and versatility. Include pieces that align with the type of work you want to attract.

3. Organize and Structure:

- ***Order Strategically***: Arrange your work logically, often starting with your strongest piece to grab the viewer's attention. Consider organizing by project type, chronology, or theme.

- ***Clear Navigation***: Ensure your portfolio is easy to navigate. Use intuitive labels, categories, or a table of contents to guide viewers through your work.

4. High-Quality Presentation:

- ***Professional Imagery***: Use high-resolution images and well-lit photographs of your work. Image quality matters.

- ***Consistency***: Maintain a consistent presentation style across all portfolio pieces. Use uniform image sizes, fonts, and formatting.

- ***Details and Context***: Include captions or descriptions that provide context for each piece. Explain your role, the project's goals, and any challenges you overcame.

5. Online Presence:

- ***Website***: Create a professional website to host your portfolio. Platforms like WordPress, Wix, Squarespace, or dedicated portfolio websites offer user-friendly templates.

- ***Social Media***: Utilize social media platforms like Instagram, Behance, or Dribbble to showcase your work. These can complement your website and attract a wider audience.

6. Keep It Updated:

- ***Regular Updates***: Continuously update your portfolio with your latest work. An outdated portfolio can give the impression that you're not actively engaged in your field.

- ***Remove Weak Work***: As you create new pieces, consider removing older, less relevant work to maintain a high-quality portfolio.

7. Show Your Process:

- ***Behind-the-Scenes***: Consider including sketches, drafts, or process shots that demonstrate how you approach and develop your creative projects. This can provide insight into your skills and creativity.

8. Testimonials and Recommendations:

- ***Client or Colleague Testimonials***: If available, include client testimonials or recommendations from colleagues or mentors to build trust and credibility.

9. Contact Information:

- ***Easy Accessibility***: Ensure that viewers can easily find your contact information. Include a contact page or a clear call-to-action for potential clients or employers to get in touch.

10. Personal Branding:

- ***Consistent Branding***: Align your portfolio's design and branding with your personal or professional brand. This helps create a cohesive and memorable impression.

11. Copyright and Permissions:

- ***Rights and Permissions***: Ensure you have the necessary rights and permissions to display each piece in your portfolio, especially if it involves client work.

12. Test Your Portfolio:

- ***Usability Testing***: Ask friends or colleagues to navigate your portfolio and provide feedback on its user-friendliness and impact.

13. Presentation Skills:

- ***In-Person Presentations***: If you anticipate in-person presentations, practice discussing your work and portfolio with confidence and clarity.

Remember that your creative portfolio is a dynamic tool that should evolve along with your skills and career. Continuously seek feedback, update it regularly, and adapt it to your changing goals and aspirations. A well-crafted portfolio can be your most compelling calling card in the world of creative professions.

Bootstrapping vs. External Funding

Bootstrapping is the practice of funding your creative business using your personal savings and revenue generated by the business itself. It's a self-sustaining approach that allows you to maintain full control and ownership but may limit the scale of your business initially.

External Funding, on the other hand, involves raising capital from sources outside your business, such as investors, loans, or grants. While it can provide the financial resources needed for growth, it often requires giving up a degree of ownership or taking on debt.

Here are the key considerations for each approach:

Bootstrapping:

Pros:
Full control and ownership.
No need to repay loans or give up equity.
Focus on profitability from the start.

Cons:
Limited initial resources.
Slower growth potential.
Personal financial risk.
External Funding:

Pros:
Access to significant capital for growth.
Faster scaling and expansion opportunities.

Expertise and mentorship from investors.

Cons:
Loss of ownership or equity.
Debt obligations and repayment.
Pressure to meet investor expectations.

The choice between bootstrapping and seeking external funding depends on your business goals, risk tolerance, and growth ambitions. Some creative entrepreneurs opt for a combination of both approaches, starting with bootstrapping and later seeking external funding to accelerate growth.

Funding Options for Creative Businesses

- ***Personal Savings***: Using your own savings is a common way to bootstrap a creative venture. It allows you to maintain full ownership and control while minimizing financial risk.

- ***<u>Friends and Family</u>***: You can seek investment from friends or family members who believe in your creative vision. However, it's important to formalize such arrangements with clear terms and agreements.

- ***<u>Crowdfunding</u>***: Platforms like Kickstarter and Indiegogo enable you to raise funds from a large number of individuals who support your creative project or product. In return, backers often receive rewards or early access.

- ***<u>Angel Investors</u>***: Angel investors are individuals who provide capital to early-stage businesses, including creative ventures. They may offer expertise and mentorship in addition to funding.

- ***<u>Venture Capital</u>***: If your creative business has high growth potential and scalability, venture capital firms may provide substantial funding in exchange for equity. Be prepared for a rigorous due diligence process.

- ***Bank Loans***: Traditional bank loans, including business loans and lines of credit, are an option for securing capital, but they often require collateral and a strong credit history.

- ***Grants and Competitions***: Many organizations and government agencies offer grants and competitions specifically for creative businesses. These can provide non-dilutive funding.

- ***Strategic Partnerships***: Collaborate with other businesses or organizations in your industry for funding and resources. These partnerships can also open up new market opportunities.

- ***Revenue-Based Financing***: Some companies offer revenue-based financing, where you repay the investment as a percentage of your future revenue. It can be a flexible option for creative businesses.

- ***Accelerators and Incubators***: Joining a business accelerator or incubator program can provide funding, mentorship, and access to resources to help your creative business grow.

- ***Creative Residencies and Fellowships***: Certain institutions and organizations offer creative residencies and fellowships, which provide funding and support for artists and creators to work on their projects.

When seeking external funding, it's crucial to have a well-prepared business plan, financial projections, and a clear understanding of how the funds will be used to advance your creative venture. Additionally, consider the long-term implications of each funding option on your creative business's ownership and control.

Ultimately, the funding path you choose should align with your creative vision and business objectives, whether that involves starting small and bootstrapping your way up or seeking external funding to accelerate growth and scale your creative enterprise.

Chapter 8: Crafting a Creative Portfolio

- Showcasing Your Work
- Leveraging Online Platforms
- The Power of Networking

A creative portfolio is your visual resume, a curated collection of your best work, and a powerful tool for showcasing your talent and expertise to potential clients, employers, or collaborators. In this chapter, we'll explore the importance of creating a compelling portfolio, the strategies for showcasing your work effectively, leveraging online platforms, and harnessing the power of networking to boost your creative career.

Showcasing Your Work

A well-crafted portfolio is a testament to your skills and creativity. It's your opportunity to make a lasting impression. Here's how to effectively showcase your work:

- **_Quality over Quantity:_** Select your best work for inclusion in your portfolio. A smaller selection of high-quality pieces is more impactful than a large, mediocre collection.

- **_Diversity of Work:_** Showcase a range of projects that highlight your versatility and expertise. Include projects that demonstrate your ability to solve different creative challenges.

- **_Storytelling_**: Arrange your portfolio in a way that tells a compelling story about your creative journey. Consider using captions or descriptions to provide context for each project.

- **_Consistency_**: Maintain a consistent style and aesthetic throughout your portfolio.

This creates a cohesive and professional impression.

- ***<u>Before and After</u>***: If applicable, include "before and after" examples to demonstrate your transformational skills and the impact of your work.

- ***<u>Case Studies:</u>*** Consider adding case studies that provide insight into your creative process, challenges faced, and solutions developed. Case studies offer depth and authenticity.

- ***<u>Digital and Physical</u>***: Depending on your field, you may create both digital and physical portfolios. Ensure that both formats are equally impressive.

- ***<u>Update Regularly</u>***: Keep your portfolio up to date with your latest work. Regular updates show that you are actively engaged in your craft.

Leveraging Online Platforms

In today's digital age, online platforms offer unprecedented opportunities to showcase your creative portfolio to a global audience. Here's how to make the most of digital platforms:

- **Website**: Create a professional website to host your portfolio. Choose a clean and user-friendly design that focuses on your work.

- **Online Portfolios**: Utilize online portfolio platforms like Behance, Dribbble, or Adobe Portfolio to showcase your work. These platforms are designed for creatives and offer exposure to a vast community.

- **Social Media**: Share your work on social media platforms like Instagram, Pinterest, and LinkedIn. Use relevant hashtags and engage with your audience to expand your reach.

- **Blogging**: Consider starting a blog where you can share insights, behind-the-scenes glimpses, and in-depth articles related to your creative projects.

- **Online Marketplaces**: If you create digital art, illustrations, or design templates, platforms like Etsy or Shutterstock can help you sell your work.

- **Search Engine Optimization (SEO):** Optimize your online content for search engines. This will help potential clients or employers find your portfolio when searching for specific services or skills.

The Power of Networking

Networking is a fundamental aspect of advancing your creative career. Building meaningful connections can lead to collaborations, job opportunities, and invaluable advice. Here's how to harness the power of networking:

- **<u>Attend Events</u>**: Attend industry events, conferences, workshops, and meetups. These gatherings provide opportunities to meet like-minded professionals and potential clients.

- **<u>Online Communities</u>**: Join online forums, groups, and social media communities related to your creative niche. Engage in discussions, share your work, and seek advice.

- **<u>Collaborate</u>**: Collaborate with other creatives on projects. Collaboration not only enhances your portfolio but also expands your network.

- **<u>Mentorship</u>**: Seek out mentors or experienced professionals in your field. Their guidance can be invaluable in your creative journey.

- **<u>Follow Up</u>**: After meeting someone at an event or online, follow up with a personalized message or email. Building and nurturing relationships requires ongoing communication.

- **<u>Give Back:</u>** Be willing to help others in your network. Sharing your knowledge and expertise can strengthen your connections and reputation.

- **<u>Professional Organizations</u>**: Join professional organizations or associations in your field. These organizations often offer networking events and resources for members.

Your creative portfolio, whether in a physical or digital format, is a dynamic representation of your skills and creative journey. It serves as a testament to your abilities and opens doors to new opportunities. Leveraging online platforms and networking effectively can amplify the impact of your portfolio, helping you connect with clients, collaborators, and mentors who can propel your creative career to new heights.

Chapter 9: Marketing and Promotion

- Digital Marketing for Creatives
- Content Marketing Strategies
- Building an Engaged Community

Marketing and promotion are essential aspects of growing your creative business and reaching your target audience. In this chapter, we will explore digital marketing strategies tailored to creatives, effective content marketing strategies, and the art of building an engaged community around your creative brand. In this section, we will delve deeper into various aspects of marketing and promotion for creatives.

Understanding Your Target Audience

Before embarking on a marketing and promotion journey, it's crucial to have a clear understanding of your target audience.

Ask yourself:

1. Who is your ideal customer or client? Define their demographics, interests, and needs.

2. What problems or desires does your creative work address? Identify the pain points your work can solve or the aspirations it can fulfill.

3. Where does your target audience spend their time online and offline? Know which platforms and spaces they frequent.

4. What motivates and influences their purchasing decisions? Understand the factors that drive them to choose one creative product or service over another.

Crafting Your Unique Selling Proposition (USP)

Your Unique Selling Proposition is what sets you apart from your competitors and gives your creative business a competitive edge. It's the essence of your brand and what makes your work special. When developing your USP:

- **Highlight Your Strengths**: Emphasize your unique skills, expertise, or style that makes your work stand out.

- **<u>Solve a Problem</u>**: Showcase how your creative work addresses specific problems or fulfills particular needs within your niche.

- **<u>Tell Your Story:</u>** Share the story behind your creative journey. Personal narratives can be compelling USPs.

- **<u>Quality and Consistency</u>**: Commit to delivering consistent quality in your creative products or services.

<u>Creating Compelling Content</u>

Content creation is at the core of modern marketing. Here are some content strategies for creatives:

- **Portfolio Showcase**: Continually update and curate your online portfolio to display your best work.

- **<u>Blogs and Articles</u>**: Write about topics related to your creative niche. Share your insights, experiences, and industry knowledge.

- **<u>Visual Content:</u>** Leverage your creative skills to produce visually engaging content for platforms like Instagram, Pinterest, and YouTube.

- **<u>Email Marketing</u>**: Build an email list and send regular newsletters, updates, and exclusive content to your subscribers.

- **<u>Video Content:</u>** Consider creating video content to showcase your creative process, tutorials, or behind-the-scenes glimpses.

- **<u>Webinars and Workshops</u>**: Host online events where you can connect with your audience in real-time, share knowledge, and answer questions.

<u>Social Media Marketing</u>

Social media platforms offer powerful tools for promoting your creative work:

- **<u>Choose the Right Platforms</u>**: Select social media platforms that align with your target audience and creative niche.

- **<u>Consistency is Key</u>**: Maintain a consistent posting schedule to keep your audience engaged.

- **<u>Engage with Your Audience</u>**: Respond to comments, messages, and feedback to foster meaningful connections.

- **<u>Visual Storytelling</u>**: Utilize storytelling techniques to engage and captivate your audience.

- **<u>Paid Advertising</u>**: Consider using paid advertising on platforms like Facebook, Instagram, or Pinterest to reach a broader audience.

Collaborations and Networking

Collaborating with other creatives, influencers, or businesses in your niche can expand your reach and introduce your work to new audiences. Attend industry events, join online communities, and network both online and offline to build valuable connections.

Measuring and Adjusting Your Marketing Efforts

Track the performance of your marketing campaigns using key performance indicators (KPIs) relevant to your goals. Analyze metrics like website traffic, social media engagement, email open rates, and sales conversion rates. Use this data to make informed adjustments to your marketing strategy for continuous improvement.

Remember that effective marketing and promotion require ongoing effort and adaptation. As you build your brand presence and connect with your target audience, you'll see the positive impact on your creative business's growth and success.

Digital Marketing for Creatives

Digital marketing is a versatile and powerful tool for creatives to showcase their work, attract clients, and build their brand online. Here are key digital marketing strategies for creatives:

- **Website Optimization**: Ensure your website is user-friendly, mobile-responsive, and optimized for search engines (SEO). Use keywords relevant to your creative niche to improve discoverability.

- **Social Media Presence**: Utilize social media platforms such as Instagram, Facebook, Pinterest, and LinkedIn to showcase your work, engage with your audience, and connect with potential clients or collaborators.

- **<u>Email Marketing</u>**: Build and nurture an email list of interested prospects and clients. Send regular newsletters featuring your latest work, insights, and promotions.

- **Online Advertising**: Consider paid advertising on platforms like Google Ads or social media advertising to reach a broader audience. Target your ads based on demographics and interests.

- **Content Creation**: Produce high-quality content relevant to your creative niche. This can include blog posts, videos, podcasts, or infographics that provide value to your audience.

- **Online Marketplaces**: List your creative products or services on online marketplaces like Etsy, Behance, or Fiverr to expand your reach and gain visibility.

- **Influencer Collaborations:** Collaborate with influencers or industry leaders who align with your brand. Their endorsement can introduce your work to a broader audience.

- **Online Portfolio**: Create an impressive online portfolio that showcases your best work, testimonials, and case studies. This acts as a digital showcase for potential clients or employers.

Content Marketing Strategies

Content marketing involves creating and distributing valuable content to attract and engage your target audience. Effective content marketing strategies for creatives include:

- **Blogging**: Maintain a blog on your website where you share insights, tutorials, industry news, and stories related to your creative field.

- **Visual Content**: As a creative, visual content is your forte. Share your work, creative process, and behind-the-scenes glimpses on platforms like Instagram, Pinterest, or YouTube.

- **Guest Posting**: Write guest posts for relevant blogs, websites, or publications in your niche. This can help you reach new audiences and establish authority.

- **Ebooks and Guides**: Create informative ebooks or guides that provide value to your audience. Offer them as downloadable resources in exchange for email sign-ups.

- **Video Content**: Leverage video content, such as tutorials, time-lapse videos of your creative process, or studio tours. Video can be particularly engaging for visual artists and craftspeople.

- **Webinars and Workshops**: Host webinars or online workshops to share your expertise and connect with your audience in real-time.

- **Podcasting**: If your niche allows, consider starting a podcast where you discuss industry trends, interview experts, or share creative stories.

Building an Engaged Community

Building a community around your creative brand is an effective way to foster engagement and loyalty. Here's how to create and maintain an engaged community:

- **Engage Authentically**: Respond to comments, messages, and feedback promptly. Show genuine interest in your community's thoughts and ideas.

- **Consistency**: Maintain a consistent posting schedule on your chosen platforms to keep your audience engaged.

- **Collaborate**: Collaborate with other creatives or businesses in your niche. Joint projects or events can help cross-promote and build community.

- **Exclusive Content**: Offer exclusive content or perks to your most loyal followers or subscribers. This can include early access, discounts, or special events.

- **Interactive Content:** Host contests, polls, Q&A sessions, or challenges to encourage active participation from your community.

- **Storytelling**: Share personal stories and experiences related to your creative journey. Authentic storytelling can resonate deeply with your audience.

- **Feedback and Surveys:** Seek feedback and input from your community. Use surveys or polls to involve them in decision-making and improve your offerings.

Remember that building a community takes time and effort. Nurture your relationships with your audience and continuously provide value to keep them engaged and invested in your creative journey.

In this chapter, you've explored digital marketing strategies, effective content marketing tactics, and community-building techniques tailored to creatives. By implementing these strategies, you can expand your reach, engage with your audience, and build a strong and loyal community around your creative brand.

Chapter 10: Sales and Pricing Strategies

- Setting the Right Prices
- Sales Techniques for Creatives
- Handling Rejection and Negotiation

Sales and pricing strategies are essential components of any successful creative business. In this chapter, we will explore how to set the right prices for your creative products or services, effective sales techniques tailored to creatives, and how to handle rejection and negotiation in the sales process. Here, we'll delve into the nuances of setting the right prices for your creative products or services and explore effective sales strategies tailored to the creative industry.

Setting the Right Prices

Pricing your creative work appropriately is essential for profitability and the perceived value of your offerings. Here are key steps to guide you in setting the right prices:

- ***Cost Analysis***: Calculate all the costs associated with producing your creative products or services. Include materials, labor, overhead, and any other expenses.

- ***Market Research***: Research your niche and competition to understand the price range for similar products or services. Analyze the pricing strategies of your competitors.

- ***Value-Based Pricing***: Consider the unique value your creative work provides to clients or customers. Price based on the perceived value and benefits rather than just covering costs.

- ***Positioning***: Determine where you want your creative business to be positioned in the market. Are you aiming for a luxury, mid-range, or budget-friendly segment? Price accordingly.

- ***Pricing Models***: Explore various pricing models, such as hourly rates, project-based pricing, subscription models, or tiered pricing. Choose the model that aligns with your business goals.

- ***Experiment and Adjust***: Be open to experimenting with pricing. Monitor how changes affect sales and profitability, and adapt your pricing strategy as needed.

- ***Value-Added Services:*** Consider offering value-added services or packages that can justify higher prices. Show clients or customers the extra benefits they'll receive.

- ***Discounts and Promotions***: Use discounts and promotions strategically to attract new clients or customers. However, be cautious not to devalue your work by offering discounts too frequently.

Sales Techniques for Creatives

Effective sales techniques are essential for converting leads into paying clients or customers. Here are some strategies tailored to the creative industry:

- ***Relationship Building***: Establish trust and build genuine relationships with potential clients or customers. Show a sincere interest in their needs and aspirations.

- ***Consultative Selling***: Listen actively to your clients or customers, understanding their pain points. Offer tailored solutions that address their specific needs and challenges.

- ***Storytelling***: Share your creative journey and the stories behind your work.

Storytelling can create emotional connections that lead to sales.

- ***Effective Communication***: Clearly and persuasively communicate the unique value and benefits of your creative work. Show how it can meet the client's or customer's needs.

- ***Overcoming Objections***: Be prepared to address objections or concerns that potential clients or customers may have. Offer solutions and provide reassurance.

- ***Closing the Sale***: When the time is right, confidently ask for the sale. Be transparent about the terms and what the client or customer can expect.

Handling Rejection and Negotiation

Rejection is a part of the sales process, and negotiation skills are essential for creative professionals. Here's how to handle rejection and negotiation effectively:

- **Resilience**: Develop resilience and understand that rejection is not a reflection of your worth as a creative professional.

- **Feedback**: When possible, seek feedback from potential clients or customers who chose not to buy. Use this feedback to improve your sales approach.

- **Positive Mindset**: Maintain a positive mindset and focus on the next opportunity rather than dwelling on rejection.

- **Negotiation Skills:** When negotiating with clients or customers, be flexible and willing to find win-win solutions. Understand their needs and constraints.

- ***Setting Boundaries***: Know your limits and the minimum acceptable terms for a sale. Don't compromise to the point where it negatively impacts your business.

- ***Follow-Up***: Stay in touch with potential clients or customers who didn't make an immediate purchase. They may be interested at a later time.

Effective sales and pricing strategies are pivotal for the success of your creative business. By setting the right prices, employing effective sales techniques, and handling rejection and negotiation with confidence and professionalism, you can enhance your ability to attract clients or customers and achieve your business goals.

Effective sales and pricing strategies are crucial for the success of your creative business. By setting the right prices, employing effective sales techniques, and handling rejection and negotiation with confidence and professionalism, you can enhance your ability to attract clients or customers and achieve your business goals.

Chapter 11: Customer Relationship Management

- Building Strong Client Relationships
- Handling Feedback and Criticism

Customer relationship management is a critical aspect of running a successful creative business. In this chapter, we'll explore strategies for building strong client relationships and effectively handling feedback and criticism.

Building Strong Client Relationships

- ***Communication***: Effective communication is the cornerstone of a strong client relationship. Maintain open lines of communication from the initial contact through project completion and beyond. Listen actively to your clients, ask questions, and provide regular updates on project progress.

- ***Clear Expectations***: Set clear expectations from the beginning. Define project scope, timelines, deliverables, and costs in writing. This helps prevent misunderstandings and disputes later on.

- ***Transparency***: Be transparent about your creative process, including any potential challenges or delays. Clients appreciate honesty and transparency.

- ***Quality and Consistency***: Consistently deliver high-quality work. Consistency builds trust and confidence in your creative abilities.

- ***Respect and Professionalism***: Treat your clients with respect and professionalism at all times. Address their concerns promptly and professionally.

- ***Timeliness***: Honor deadlines and commitments. Timely delivery of work demonstrates reliability and commitment to your clients.

- ***Personalization:*** Take the time to understand your clients' unique needs and preferences. Tailor your creative solutions to meet their specific requirements.

- ***Feedback and Updates:*** Request feedback from clients throughout the project. Keep them updated on progress and involve them in decision-making when appropriate.

- ***Exceed Expectations:*** Whenever possible, go the extra mile to exceed client expectations. Surprise and delight clients with exceptional service and results.

- ***Post-Project Follow-Up:*** After project completion, follow up with clients to ensure their satisfaction and inquire about opportunities for improvement.

Handling Feedback and Criticism

- ***Open Mindset***: Approach feedback and criticism with an open mindset. View them as opportunities for growth and improvement rather than as personal attacks.

- ***Listen Actively***: When receiving feedback, listen actively without interrupting. Allow the person to express their thoughts and concerns fully.

- ***Thank You:*** Express gratitude for feedback, even if it's critical. Thank the person for taking the time to share their thoughts.

- ***Seek Clarification:*** If feedback is unclear or vague, seek clarification to ensure you understand the specific issues or concerns.

- ***Reflect and Learn:*** Reflect on the feedback and consider how it can be used to improve your work or processes. Be open to making necessary changes.

- ***Respond Calmly:*** If responding to criticism, do so calmly and professionally. Avoid becoming defensive or confrontational.

- ***Implement Changes:*** If feedback highlights valid issues, take proactive steps to implement changes and improvements.

- ***Feedback Loop***: Encourage ongoing feedback from clients and colleagues to continuously refine your creative work and processes.

- ***Constructive Criticism***: When providing feedback to others, offer constructive criticism that is specific, actionable, and respectful.

- ***Self-Reflection***: Periodically engage in self-reflection and self-assessment to identify areas where you can improve and grow as a creative professional.

Remember that constructive feedback is a valuable tool for personal and professional development. Embrace it as an opportunity to refine your skills, enhance your offerings, and strengthen your client relationships.

Chapter 12: Scaling and Growth

- Expanding Your Creative Business
- Managing Growth Challenges

Scaling and growth are pivotal phases in the life of a creative business. In this chapter, we'll explore strategies for expanding your creative business and managing the challenges that come with growth.

Expanding Your Creative Business

- ***Diversification***: Consider diversifying your creative offerings to appeal to a broader audience. Explore new creative niches, products, or services that align with your expertise.

- ***Leverage Your Brand***: Capitalize on the reputation and brand you've built. Use your existing client base and loyal following to introduce new products or services.

- ***Collaborations and Partnerships***: Collaborate with other creatives, businesses, or influencers in your niche. Partnerships can help you reach new audiences and expand your market presence.

- ***Online Presence***: Invest in a robust online presence. A well-designed website, active social media presence, and engaging content can attract a larger audience.

- ***Market Expansion:*** Explore new geographic markets or target demographics that may be interested in your creative work.

- ***Hiring and Outsourcing***: As your workload increases, consider hiring additional team members or outsourcing tasks to freelancers or agencies to maintain high-quality service.

- ***Automation and Technology***: Utilize automation tools and technology to streamline processes, reduce administrative tasks, and improve efficiency.

- ***Customer Loyalty Programs***: Implement customer loyalty programs to retain existing clients and incentivize repeat business.

Managing Growth Challenges

- ***Scaling Financially***: Ensure you have the financial resources to support growth. Budget for increased expenses, such as additional staff or marketing efforts, and monitor cash flow carefully.

- ***Operational Efficiency***: Optimize your operational processes to handle increased demand efficiently. Consider investing in project management tools or software to manage workflows.

- ***Quality Control***: Maintain strict quality control standards as you grow. Consistency in delivering high-quality work is vital to retaining clients and reputation.

- ***Client Relationships***: Continue to prioritize strong client relationships. As your business expands, it's easy to lose the personal touch with clients. Implement strategies to ensure client satisfaction and maintain communication.

- ***Scalable Systems***: Build scalable systems that can accommodate growth. This includes flexible workflows, standardized procedures, and scalable technology infrastructure.

- ***Risk Management***: Identify potential risks associated with growth, such as increased competition or changing market dynamics. Develop strategies to mitigate these risks.

- ***Legal and Compliance***: Ensure that your business complies with all relevant legal and regulatory requirements as you expand into new markets or offer new services.

- ***Employee Development***: If you hire employees, invest in their development and provide training to ensure they can meet the demands of a growing business.

- ***Market Research***: Continuously conduct market research to stay updated on industry trends and changing customer preferences. This information can guide your growth strategies.

- ***Adaptability***: Stay adaptable and open to change. The business landscape is dynamic, and your ability to adapt to new challenges and opportunities is crucial for sustained growth.

Scaling and growing a creative business can be both rewarding and challenging. By strategically expanding your offerings, maintaining a focus on quality and client relationships, and effectively managing the challenges that come with growth, you can position your creative business for long-term success.

Chapter 13: Overcoming Creative Blocks and Burnout

- The Creative Process
- Dealing with Burnout
- Staying Inspired

The creative process is a journey filled with moments of inspiration, innovation, and artistic fulfillment. Yet, it's also marked by challenges, including creative blocks and burnout. In this chapter, we'll explore the creative process, effective strategies for dealing with burnout, and ways to stay inspired.

The Creative Process

The creative process is a dynamic and often nonlinear journey that artists, writers, designers, and creators of all kinds embark upon. While it may differ from person to person, it generally encompasses several stages:

- **<u>Inspiration</u>**: This is the spark that ignites your creativity. It can come from anywhere—a fleeting thought, a conversation, nature, or a piece of art. Inspiration is the fuel that drives the creative process.

- **<u>Ideation</u>**: During this stage, you generate and refine ideas. It involves brainstorming, research, and experimentation. It's about exploring possibilities and shaping your initial inspiration into a concrete concept.

- **<u>Creation</u>**: Here, you bring your ideas to life. Whether you're painting, writing, designing, or crafting, this stage involves the actual production of your creative work. It can be both exhilarating and challenging.

- **Revision and Refinement**: Rarely does a creative project emerge fully formed. Revision and refinement are essential steps where you review and improve your work. It's a process of critique and enhancement.

- **Completion**: This is the moment when you finish your creative project and present it to the world. It can be a deeply satisfying stage, but it can also trigger feelings of vulnerability and self-doubt.

- **Feedback and Iteration**: After sharing your work, you may receive feedback. Use this input to refine your work further. The creative process often involves multiple iterations before a project reaches its final form.

Dealing with Burnout

Creativity is a powerful but finite resource. Burnout can strike when you've overextended yourself or when you're grappling with creative blocks. Here's how to address burnout effectively:

- **<u>Self-Care</u>**: Prioritize self-care to nurture your physical and mental well-being. Get enough sleep, eat healthily, exercise regularly, and practice relaxation techniques.

- **<u>Set Boundaries</u>**: Establish clear boundaries between work and personal life. Overworking can lead to burnout. Create a schedule that allows for downtime and relaxation.

- **<u>Creative Rest</u>**: If you're facing creative burnout, take a break from your usual creative pursuits. Engage in activities that refresh your mind, like reading, taking walks, or exploring new hobbies.

- **<u>Mindfulness and Meditation</u>**: Mindfulness practices can help reduce stress and promote mental clarity.

Meditation can be a valuable tool for recharging your creative energy.

- **Seek Support**: Talk to friends, family, or a therapist about your feelings of burnout. Sometimes, sharing your emotions and seeking support can alleviate the burden.

- **Set Realistic Goals**: Avoid overcommitting. Set achievable creative goals and deadlines. Unrealistic expectations can contribute to burnout.

Staying Inspired

Maintaining a consistent flow of inspiration is vital for overcoming creative blocks and burnout:

- **Curiosity**: Cultivate a curious mindset. Explore new topics, art forms, or cultures. Learning something new can trigger fresh inspiration.

- **<u>Creative Rituals</u>**: Establish rituals or routines that signal to your brain that it's time to be creative. This could be as simple as lighting a candle or listening to specific music.

- **<u>Change of Environment</u>**: Sometimes, changing your physical surroundings can stimulate creativity. Work in a different space or take a day trip to a new location for fresh perspectives.

- **<u>Collaboration</u>**: Collaborating with other creatives can be highly inspiring. Sharing ideas and perspectives often leads to new creative insights.

- **<u>Mood Boards and Journals</u>**: Create mood boards, scrapbooks, or journals where you collect images, quotes, and ideas that resonate with you. These can serve as wellsprings of inspiration.

- **<u>Mind Mapping</u>**: Use mind mapping techniques to visually explore and connect ideas. It can help you discover unexpected connections and insights.

- **<u>Nature and Solitude</u>**: Spend time in nature or in solitude. These environments often provide a fertile ground for deep thinking and creative breakthroughs.

Chapter 14: Sustainability and Social Responsibility

- Ethical Business Practices
- Sustainability in the Creative Industry

In an era of increasing environmental awareness and ethical considerations, creatives must embrace sustainability and social responsibility. Let's delve into ethical business practices and sustainability in the creative industry.

Ethical Business Practices

- **Transparency**: Be transparent with your clients and customers about your business practices. This includes pricing, sourcing of materials, and any potential environmental or social impacts.

- **Fair Wages**: Ensure fair wages and working conditions for yourself and any employees or collaborators. Ethical treatment of everyone involved in your creative process is paramount.

- **Respect for Intellectual Property**: Respect the intellectual property rights of others. Use copyrighted materials or designs only with proper authorization or under fair use provisions.

- **Honest Marketing**: Avoid deceptive or misleading marketing tactics. Provide accurate information about your products or services.

- **Sustainability**: Prioritize sustainable materials and processes whenever possible. Consider the environmental impact of your work, and seek eco-friendly alternatives.

Sustainability in the Creative Industry

- **Eco-Friendly Materials**: Opt for eco-friendly materials, such as recycled paper or sustainable textiles, in your creative projects. Reducing waste is a crucial step in sustainability.

- **Reduce, Reuse, Recycle**: Embrace the principles of reduce, reuse, and recycle in your creative process. Find ways to repurpose materials and minimize waste.

- **Carbon Footprint**: Assess and reduce your carbon footprint. Consider sustainable transportation options and offset your emissions when necessary.

- **Local Sourcing**: Whenever possible, source materials locally to support local economies and reduce the environmental impact of transportation.

- **Minimal Packaging**: Minimize excessive packaging and consider sustainable packaging materials. Encourage clients to recycle or repurpose packaging.

- **Education and Advocacy**: Educate yourself and others in your creative community about sustainability. Advocate for sustainable practices within your industry.

By integrating ethical practices and sustainability into your creative business, you not only contribute to a better world but also align your brand with the values of an increasingly conscious consumer base. Creativity and responsibility can coexist harmoniously, creating a positive impact on your work and the world around you.

Chapter 15: Navigating Challenges and Adversities

- Common Challenges for Creative Entrepreneurs
- Resilience and Adaptation

Creative entrepreneurship is a rewarding journey, but it's not without its share of challenges and adversities. In this chapter, we'll explore the common challenges faced by creative entrepreneurs, the importance of resilience and adaptation, and strategies to overcome obstacles.

Common Challenges for Creative Entrepreneurs

- **Financial Instability:** Irregular income streams, fluctuating demand, and unpredictable project timelines can lead to financial instability.

- **Self-Doubt and Creative Blocks:** Creativity often goes hand in hand with self-doubt and creative blocks. These mental hurdles can hinder productivity and confidence.

- **Competition**: The creative industry is highly competitive, and standing out in a crowded marketplace can be challenging.

- **Client Relations**: Managing client expectations, dealing with difficult clients, and maintaining healthy client relationships can be stressful.

- **Balancing Creativity and Business:** Creative entrepreneurs must juggle their artistic pursuits with the demands of running a business, which requires a different skill set.

- **Marketing and Promotion:** Effective marketing and self-promotion are essential but can be intimidating for those with limited marketing experience.

- **Work-Life Balance:** The boundary between work and personal life can blur, leading to burnout and strained relationships.

- **Legal and Intellectual Property Issues:** Navigating intellectual property rights, contracts, and legal matters can be complex and time-consuming.

Resilience and Adaptation

Resilience is the ability to bounce back from setbacks and adversities. Creative entrepreneurs often rely on their resilience to overcome challenges. Here's how to cultivate resilience:

- **Mindset**: Cultivate a growth mindset, which embraces challenges as opportunities for learning and growth.

- **Self-Care**: Prioritize self-care to maintain physical and mental well-being. A healthy body and mind are better equipped to handle challenges.

- **Support System**: Build a support network of fellow creatives, mentors, or friends who can provide guidance and encouragement.

- **Adaptability**: Be open to change and adaptable. The ability to pivot and adjust strategies is essential in a dynamic marketplace.

- **Problem-Solving**: Develop problem-solving skills. Break challenges into smaller, manageable steps and approach them systematically.

- **Learn from Failure**: Failure is a natural part of entrepreneurship. Instead of dwelling on it, extract lessons and use them to improve.

- **Goal Setting**: Set clear, achievable goals. Goals provide direction and motivation during challenging times.

Chapter 16: Success Stories: Creative Entrepreneurs in Action

- Inspiring Case Studies
- Lessons from Successful Creative Entrepreneurs

Success stories of creative entrepreneurs inspire and provide valuable insights. In this chapter, we'll delve into inspiring case studies and lessons from successful creative entrepreneurs.

Inspiring Case Studies

- **Steve Jobs and Apple**: Steve Jobs' relentless pursuit of innovation revolutionized the tech industry. Apple's story showcases the power of visionary leadership and a commitment to excellence.

- **J.K. Rowling:** J.K. Rowling's journey from struggling writer to the creator of the Harry Potter series is a testament to perseverance and the enduring appeal of storytelling.

- **Walt Disney**: Walt Disney's pioneering work in animation and theme park design laid the foundation for one of the world's most iconic entertainment companies.

- **Oprah Winfrey**: Oprah's rise from a challenging upbringing to a media mogul and philanthropist highlights the importance of authenticity and resilience.

- **Elon Musk:** Elon Musk's ventures, including Tesla and SpaceX, demonstrate how audacious goals and a relentless pursuit of innovation can reshape entire industries.

Lessons from Successful Creative Entrepreneurs

- **Passion and Purpose**: Successful creatives are often deeply passionate about their work and driven by a sense of purpose.

- **Resilience**: They demonstrate resilience in the face of adversity, viewing failures as stepping stones toward success.

- **Innovation**: Creativity and innovation are at the core of their endeavors, constantly pushing boundaries and challenging the status quo.

- **Adaptability**: They adapt to changing circumstances and embrace new opportunities, even if it means stepping outside their comfort zone.

- **<u>Persistence</u>**: Perseverance is a common trait among successful creative entrepreneurs. They keep going even when faced with setbacks.

- **<u>Community and Collaboration:</u>** Building a supportive network and collaborating with others are keys to their success.

Chapter 17: The Future of Creative Entrepreneurship

- Trends and Opportunities
- Preparing for an Ever-Evolving Landscape

The landscape of creative entrepreneurship is ever-evolving. In this final chapter, we'll explore emerging trends and opportunities and discuss how to prepare for an ever-changing future.

Trends and Opportunities

- **Digital Transformation**: Embrace digital tools and platforms for marketing, sales, and collaboration. The digital landscape offers vast opportunities for creative entrepreneurs.

- **Remote Work**: The rise of remote work allows creative professionals to collaborate globally and access a broader client base.

- **Sustainability**: Sustainability and eco-consciousness are increasingly important to consumers. Explore sustainable practices in your creative work.

- **Niche Markets**: Specializing in niche markets allows for targeted marketing and potentially higher profits.

- **AI and Automation**: Leverage AI and automation tools to streamline tasks and focus on creative work.

- **Diversity and Inclusion**: Embrace diversity and inclusion in your creative projects and teams, reflecting the values of an evolving society.

Preparing for an Ever-Evolving Landscape

- **<u>Continuous Learning</u>**: Stay updated with industry trends and technologies. Invest in continuous learning and skill development.

- **<u>Networking</u>**: Build a strong professional network. Collaborations and partnerships can open doors to new opportunities.

- **<u>Flexibility</u>**: Be adaptable and open to change. The ability to pivot and embrace new directions is invaluable.

- **<u>Market Research</u>**: Regularly conduct market research to identify emerging trends and evolving customer preferences.

- **<u>Resilience</u>**: Cultivate resilience to navigate challenges and setbacks with grace and determination.

- **<u>Innovation</u>**: Continue to innovate and experiment. Creative entrepreneurship thrives on fresh ideas and approaches.

Creative entrepreneurship is a dynamic and fulfilling path that requires dedication, creativity, and adaptability. By understanding the common challenges, cultivating resilience, drawing inspiration from success stories, and staying attuned to future trends, you can embark on a successful and fulfilling journey in the ever-evolving world of creative entrepreneurship.

Conclusion

- Your Creative Business Journey: Looking Ahead
- Final Words of Inspiration

As you embark on or continue your creative business journey, it's essential to reflect on the path you've traveled and look ahead to the exciting possibilities that await you. This concluding section offers final words of inspiration and encouragement.

Your Creative Business Journey

Your creative business journey is a remarkable voyage filled with artistic expression, entrepreneurial spirit, and personal growth. Along the way, you've explored the intricacies of identifying your creative skills, conducting market research, building a strong brand, and crafting a unique value proposition. You've delved into the world of legalities, funding options, and marketing strategies. You've learned how to manage client relationships, handle feedback, and navigate the challenges and adversities that creative entrepreneurship often presents.

Looking Ahead

As you look ahead on your creative business journey, keep these principles in mind:

- **Passion and Purpose**: Your passion for your creative work is a driving force. Let it guide you as you continue to create and innovate.

- **Adaptability**: Be open to change and adaptable to evolving trends and technologies. Embrace new opportunities as they arise.

- **Resilience**: Remember that challenges and setbacks are part of the journey. Your ability to bounce back and learn from these experiences is a valuable asset.

- **Collaboration**: The creative world thrives on collaboration. Seek out opportunities to work with others, share ideas, and create something beautiful together.

- **Sustainability**: Embrace sustainable practices, both in your creative work and in your business operations. Be mindful of the impact you have on the environment and society.

- **Innovation**: Continue to innovate and push the boundaries of your creativity. Explore new mediums, techniques, and ideas.

- **Community**: Build a supportive community of fellow creatives, mentors, and clients. Nurture these relationships, as they can be a source of inspiration and growth.

Final Words of Inspiration

As you conclude this journey, remember that creative entrepreneurship is not just a business; it's a way of life. It's a pursuit that allows you to blend your artistic passion with your entrepreneurial spirit, creating a unique path that is uniquely yours.

Never underestimate the power of your creativity. Your ideas, your vision, and your artistry have the potential to make a profound impact on the world. Embrace the challenges and setbacks as opportunities for growth and learning. Celebrate your successes, both big and small, and use them as stepping stones toward your next creative endeavor.

Above all, stay true to your creative voice and the values that guide your work. Your authenticity and dedication will shine through in everything you create, and it will be the driving force behind your continued success.

Your creative business journey is a story still being written. The canvas is yours, the stage is set, and the world is waiting for your next masterpiece. So, take a deep breath, embrace the future with optimism and enthusiasm, and let your creativity soar.

Congratulations on your creative business journey, and may it be filled with boundless inspiration and endless possibilities.

Acknowledgments

A creative endeavor, such as writing a book on creative entrepreneurship, is not a solitary pursuit. It involves the contributions, support, and inspiration of many individuals and resources. We would like to express our heartfelt gratitude to those who have played a significant role in bringing this book to fruition.

Our Thanks Go To:

- **God Almighty**

- **Creative Minds**: To all the creative entrepreneurs and artists who generously shared their experiences, insights, and stories. Your contributions have enriched the content of this book and inspired countless others on their entrepreneurial journeys.

- **Mentors and Advisors**: To the mentors and advisors who provided guidance, expertise, and valuable feedback throughout the writing process. Your wisdom and experience have been invaluable.

- **Readers and Supporters**: To the readers and supporters who have shown interest in this book from its inception. Your enthusiasm and encouragement have been a driving force in our commitment to creating a valuable resource.

- **Family and Friends**: To our families and friends for their unwavering support, patience, and understanding during the long hours spent crafting this book. Your belief in us has been a constant source of motivation.

- **Publishing Team**: To the publishing team, editors, and professionals who helped shape and refine this manuscript. Your expertise and dedication have

transformed ideas into a coherent
narrative.

- **The Creative Community**: To the entire
  creative community, both established and
  emerging, for your boundless creativity
  and passion. You inspire us every day.

Remember that creativity is a collaborative
endeavor, and your contributions to the world of
art and entrepreneurship are invaluable. We
hope this book serves as a source of knowledge,
inspiration, and empowerment for all creative
entrepreneurs on their remarkable journeys.

With heartfelt gratitude,

[Simeon Favour]